End

"Sit with these verses and you will find yourself connecting with words. Katherine Moore reflects that God is in this connecting. We discover that words go beyond engaging our minds and wash over us, opening silent places in our hearts ... In the section entitled 'Backyard Theology,' Katherine lets us notice such things as oak branches, coffee aroma, dismal rain, and gossamer wings, and in so doing we discover the holy. Take the journey with Katherine Moore through this meditative volume of verse, and you will experience more deeply that you are alive!"

—Jonathan Kelley, D.Min., LPC, director of the Presbyterian Counseling Center, Brunswick County, North Carolina

"Katherine Moore's collection of poems is visceral and haunting yet joyful. She reaches into her soul and shows us the frustrations and agonies of daily life, yet through it all she keeps a sense of wonder and delight ... Her poems will make you both laugh and cry. With blunt honesty, through the art of poetry, Katherine tells us how she really feels, and we instantly connect with all the things in her view."

—Elsa Bonstein, columnist, poet, writer

"This is a book to be pondered. It is a reflection of the woes and wonders that scribble divinity on the human person. The poems come from the depth of a woman's spirit and speak to the core of our humanity ... The work is indeed a 'holy scribbling' that makes us aware we are more wholly sacred than ever we imagined. Read it. Meditate with it. Take it seriously as the wisdom of a heart laid open for all and to all.

—Fran Salone-Pelletier, author of *Awakening to God: The Sunday Readings in Our Lives* and religion columnist for *The Brunswick Beacon*

To my husband,
whose patience could come
only from God

Contents

ACKNOWLEDGMENTS

For challenging me to put this book together, I wish to thank my long-time friend, Wallace Sills. I also want to extend my gratitude to the *Poetry Revisited* group in Ocean Isle Beach, NC, for giving me a forum to read my poems, and to Sandra Hicks for sharing her photograph for the poem *Moon Walk*.

In addition to the many who have nurtured my spirit over the years, I am especially grateful to the Northumbria Community for the exceptional beauty and wisdom contained within the pages of their prayer book, *Celtic Daily Prayer*.

INTRODUCTION

I have been scribbling for years. On scraps of paper. Backs of envelopes. Torn notepads. Sticky notes. Margins of newspaper. Only as I began to keep a journal did my "scribbles" begin to take form. The works included here are quite simple. I look at life. Over the years, I have learned the mystery of stopping, being still, and waiting—with pen in hand.

This book is both personal and spiritual. God is in it all—the queries, the despair, the pain, the delight. It reflects portions of my own spiritual journey as I experience this living planet. The themes and observations are for the most part universal. Yet in the last analysis, I confess I do write for myself—my own pondering, my own healing, my own worship—for writing is, after all, a therapeutic endeavor. If there should be one other soul who connects with these words, that is a pure bonus! At that point, I shall know fully that God is in the connecting!

Consider this book a resource of poetic and prayerful musings. I hope you will read them aloud with your voice and inwardly with your heart.

~ Words ~

We live in a "wordy" world. Media personalities pummel us daily with words that attempt to impress or manipulate. Everywhere, signs and screens and papers blast more words our way. Music lyrics stream continuously into our ears, rendering silence a near archaic experience.

Yet in spite of this, I love words! Words fascinate me. They intrigue me. But after awhile, I can hear no more. Words become excessive, tiresome. I run from them, struggling to hold the tension between words and silence, sounds and quiet.

And so, as I share my own words with you, I trust you will remember to stop from time to time and experience the power of the quiet.

THE BLANK PAGE

Clean and white it lays before me.

Waiting.

Open to newness—something not there before.

Ready.

Accepting all that is placed there.

Gathering.

Words and drawings
        and scribbles and musings.

Fragments of life
        drizzled and poured
        onto the open space.

The paper invites my heart.

And I respond.

COUNTRY RIDE

The empty paper stares at me,
beckoning words from my heart
that do not come.

Sights and sounds of
field and roadway bid me
gaze from the moving window
rather than attend to
my written phrases.

Gratitude comes easily today.
Country roads and country music
remind me of God's goodness
and tell me about hearts touching hearts
again and again.

Today my car is my church, and
I am bathed in an inexpressible
worship where words cannot go.

WRITING ISSUES

What is this writing about?

Thoughts assail me with
ideas and plans,
problems and solutions.
Fiercely I hurl the words onto paper,
but who will read them?

Thinking is troublesome.
Too much of it debilitates,
too little of it dulls.
And all of it is lost in the vapor
of the next thought.

So I write and write,
fearful of forgetting
yet producing nothing.
Words read by no one,
thoughts going nowhere.

Today I want to throw it all away
and build a mountainous heap of
   discarded journals,
   scribbled-on paper,
   and worn-out pens.

But I probably won't.

SILENCE AND SOUND

Slept too late.

The noise has begun.

I can't find the silence.

I wait for your whisper,

but I cannot hear it.

Already busy,

the world is too loud.

The din of ringing and beeping

and talking and bumping

and roaring and whirring

hides your sweet voice.

Slowly I learn …

when I sleep too late,

the silence escapes

and sacred words are lost

in the clatter.

ANOTHER LOSS

They used to come.
The words.
Leaping through the wrinkles
     of my brain,
Singing and prancing their way
     across my interior pages,
     seeking form.

Nice words.
Robust words.
Gutsy, howly, growly words.
Words like
     numinous and *nuance,*
     escarpment and *esplanade,*
     redolent and *recondite,*
     obdurate and *obsequious.*

All tapping their rhythm upon
     my mental paper
While rearranging themselves with
     meticulous precision,
     searching for perfection.

But where are they now—my words?

In a wild siege of boredom,
    they scurried off my page in a frenzy.
Seeking adventures more lofty,
    I suppose.
Now they randomly pirouette in
    other times and other places,
    leaving my poor mind void.

Oh, come back! Come back!

For what shall become of me
    now that my words have gone?

Mystic Dawn

In deep quiet
Before the stirring of life,
I lie in bed peering
At the earliest hint of dawn—
A mystical place where sleepy eyes
Seek signs of morning and
Shadowy fingers reach
Into my heart to touch places
Where I do not go
In the daylight.

The ache inside tells me of my loves.
In my dreams I search for them.
Always eluding me, I remain bereft.
And I've used all the words—
Words of longing and hurt and
Yearning and tears.
There they are, cast aside,
All in a pile,
Worn out from wear.

Once they served me well, but
I am tired of them now.
No, I won't use them.
Today I must find new words.
But perhaps I shall keep this old pile
In a corner somewhere ...
Just in case.

Word Power

Talk. Talk. Talk.
Words. Words. Words.
Keep them flowing!
Joke. Laugh. Entertain.
Stay in charge.
Hold the attention.
No pauses. No breaks.
No waiting. No silence.
No listening.

Funny how words
Create distance,
Shield from intimacy,
Maintain control.

We part,
And still
We are
Empty.

NOTHING LEFT TO SAY

There are no more words
        for the beautiful
Just as there are no words left
        for things catastrophic.

All the words have been used—
        over and over,
        stretched and shouted,
        underlined and emboldened
        until the hearer is weary of the
        deadening sound
        of sameness
        that never touches the
        truth of beauty
        or the horror of disaster
        or the pain of tragedy.

Too many words
        hammer humanity,
        numbing the senses.

And we stop listening.

~ Backyard Theology ~

Any window can be a sacred window. It isn't *what* one sees as much as *how* one looks at it. Observing life's comings and goings through a sacred lens discovers the "holy" in the stuff of ordinary living.

As I sit in my old kitchen, gazing from my sacred window once again, I am both startled and refreshed by this scrappy yard. The giant pecan tree, naked now save for the thick ivy covering trunk and limbs, stands with bare vines and tall cedar to allow glorious sunbeams to break through in scattered patches.

Suddenly, through the gray skies behind the pecan tree, there bursts a shining bold Light, clearing its path and resting squarely on my face. Illuminating me. Reassuring me. Healing body and soul.

And I know, O God, that you are One with our ragged world yet so far above it—immanent yet transcendent. Powerful theology discovered in my bedraggled backyard!

Simple Solitude

Just me this morning, Lord.
All by myself.
Why do I love it so,
this sitting by my window
that lets the tension fall
from me like unlocked shackles?
With visceral precision, my body
loosens as I gaze across from
tree to field to water.

Though fleeting and unstable,
the morning's contentment
settles over me gently,
and I give thanks
to God for something
so simple as this precious
window-spot.

COFFEE AND PRAYER

My cup is hot,
wrapped with both hands,
steeping in warmth.
Aromas reach my chilly soul
and all is good.

Dark coffee.
Bold.
Rich.
Pure.
Just how I like it.
Forever the perfect companion,
whether in lively relationships
or deepening solitude.

Coffee is slow.
One cannot hurry coffee.
Its mystery must be …
sipped,
savored,
pondered,
contemplated.

Reminds me of God.

WINDOW SCENES

Gazing through the dirty window,
I strain to see the fuzzy images
looking back at me.
How blurred the landscape appears,
dimmed by dried splotches of rain and dust
collected on the glass.

With squinting eyes, I wonder,
"Could that be a bluebird?"
But how would I know, for it appears
to be the flat silhouette of a
mere "gray" bird.

Dingy clouds cover the sky—or
perhaps I am peering at a clear
blue heaven through a
cloudy window.

And my mind?
I know now why my brain
is full of foggy thoughts
and indistinct images, for
this is simply what happens
when one looks at life
through a dirty window.

WATCHING HIM

He stands at the window, looking out at the world,
quietly observing what most of us miss—
a flutter of leaves from flitting warblers,
an egret sailing through the morning mist.
Loving the earth,
loving the sea,
he embraces each scrubby bush,
each reed,
each coastal tree.
Lowliest creatures elicit a grin
while he watches from the window.

It is cold now.
Inattentive eyes see all as dormant;
yet, peering deeply, he uncovers a spark,
a bud, a wiggle, a hinting breath of activity
casually overlooked by those of us with
less patience and less acuity.

Is this his prayer,
this silent seeing of quiet things?
The hidden, the obscure, enriching his
contemplation of humanity's place
tucked inside the woven web of Creation?

It is his pared-down way of watching and
listening to life's rhythms that makes his
gazing and reflecting seem limitless.

And the window summons his prayer.

Holy Rhythm

Stand in the morning light,
open to its warmth,
open to its focused rays
beaming into hearts
every morning.

Stand in the darkness of night,
open to the vastness of sky,
open to the shining stars dotting
heavenly dark, bringing rest
every night.

Holy rhythms.
Light-Dark-Light.
Wake-Sleep-Wake.
Life-Death-Life.

SEPARATION

Brown and brittle oak branch
Hangs by a single woody fiber,
Broken off from its life source.
No nourishment of food.
No life-giving water.
Disconnected.
Dying.

How like myself.
Separated from your
Life-giving food of love,
Do I not also turn dry and brittle?
Disconnected from my life source,
Am I not just like the oak branch?

For only a little while
Can I hang by my thread
Without your love,
Without your completeness.
For without being rooted and
Grounded in the Whole,
In the life-breath of your Being,
I, too, die.

Dead Tree Haunting

What is it about the dead tree
standing sleek and bare
in the center of the field
that captures me?

Lone crooked branch
still reaches outward,
beckoning my soul
to the mystery of solitude.

A mingling of sorrow and beauty
painting images in my mind
of memories long forgotten
brought to life by
the dead tree.

BROOM TREES

Little girl peering from her window
Imagined the pine tree tops
Were brooms turned upside down
With thousands of soft bristles
Sweeping clean the sky.

Today, gazing upward to scan the
Line of trees swaying about me,
I am convinced that this is
Still true.

SERENITY

Quietness awakened me
this morning as gentle mist
hovered across the water and
dawn's first light
eased through the vapor,
catching the droplets in a
glowing web of softness.
Silent.
Pure.
And today I live immersed in
complete serenity.

WINDS

Holding fast to their anchor
Tethered leaves tremble
As the winds blow and swirl.
God's breath?

Grounded beside the tree,
I, too, tremble with rushing
Winds of the Spirit.
God's breath.

THE LEAF

Single maple leaf
Sits on a layer of air.
Hanging in the wind.
Aloft and still.
Solitary.
Waiting for the
Fall.

COASTAL MYSTERY

Leaves rain down
in crazy clouds
as March wind gusts
shake the live oak branches
left nearly bare as they
wait, only briefly, for
new green to emerge.

I watch the small gold leaves
sail down, thinking,
it is all backward
how God mysteriously
programs the salty-air oaks
to think that fall
comes in the spring!

Rain and Coffee

From my window, I watch the world.

The rain has come again.
Beating bullets against the house.
Slugging stones on the roof.
Another day of storm and gray.

The rhythm of God's Creation—
      Day and night
      Wind and calm
      Heat and cold
      Sun and rain.

All weathers pass this window.

And the coffee brews with subtle dripping,
A soothing backdrop to the wild rain.
Its bold aroma surrounds me with warmth,
And I am wrapped in the very fragrance of comfort.

Coffee in hand, I stand and stare and sip.
A brisk rush of contentment floods me
As I sense my oneness with storm and all Creation.
Such is the gift of hot coffee,
And I revel in the intimacy.

Winter Rain

Cold raindrops form a linear stream
      running down each leaf
splatting hard against the
      wooden porch floor
while colorless gray enshrouds
      every piece of twig and tree
as the landscape is saturated
      with a dismal attitude of despair.

Brrr. It chills my bones.

Snow-Tree

Naked branch and limb
reach to the sky,
catching tiny flakes
as they fall.
Stark and gray,
each bare twig
is transformed
into twists and lines
coated with
sugar-dust white.

GOD AND THE WEATHERMAN

Does God laugh when the weatherman is wrong?
Surely there is a heavenly grin—an indication of
gentle amusement at our folly.
How boldly human for us to analyze, to assess,
to predict our days with assured certainty.
And how fallible we are.
Instruments and mechanisms
of all styles and intentions
pour forth buckets of information
and we believe,
only to be called back, over and over again,
to the reality of our creating God.
This God of all who shakes the skies and
opens the clouds to send us rain
when the weatherman and
his myriad of radar devices
clearly show sun.
Wait …
Is that an omnipotent chuckle I hear?

LITANY OF TRUST

When the sun blazes upon my shoulders,
You, O God, are my shade.

In the howling winds of terror and destruction,
You, O God, are my anchor.

As flooding torrents of rain pour over land and sea,
You, O God, are my higher ground.

When ice covers the earth in brutal chill,
You, O God, are my warm flame.

If the land shakes and moves from its foundations,
You, O God, are my solid rock.

When fire ravages homes and forests,
You, O God, are my quenching rain.

All is in you, my God.
In all my fears,
In all weathers,
In all seasons,
I place my trust in you.

May I ever remember
that I hide in the shadow
of your wings, O God.

You encircle me
with your arms
and I am not afraid.

Secure in your love
my soul is at rest.

Amen.

MORNING MUSIC

Listen to the cacophony of dawn!

I had quite forgotten how raucous,
how exciting,
how expectant
are the sounds of early morn.

All of God's creatures
sing in a harmonious frenzy,
preparing for their day.

Melody and harmony,
Solo and discord.
Each note a part of a
Masterful composition.

Surely, this is the joy of the Lord!

Shhhh.

Just listen.

DRAGON FLY

I see you,
delicate creature
with gossamer wings
spread full,
as you rest there
on my window screen.

Eye-to-eye
we encounter
one another
while I imagine
how it must be
to peer into my
human face
just as I stare back
into your great
green eyes.

THE BLUEBIRD SHOW

The bluebird show takes place
outside my window.
Captured by the zipping and skittering,
I sit and watch, transfixed,
as lapis wings flit and
dance across the narrow
strip of yard.

How many?
I get lost in the counting.
Six? Seven? Twelve?

Tangerine breasts
catch the sunlight,
and with a succession of twirls,
shining cobalt jackets
dart gaily to the
rhythm of the wind.

In a bursting flurry of
dashing spins and merriment,
the dance ends
as abruptly as it began.
The performance is over.

In awed silence,
I am left gazing onto
the empty stage.

I stand and applaud.

Fragrant Memories

Lifting their white heads to catch

    the midday sun,

Gardenias bloom outside

    my window,

Releasing their delicate sweetness

    in every jostling breeze.

I inhale the heady fragrance and close

    my eyes with

Lovely memories of lost days of

    soft summer air

    and home.

WAVES

salty waves thunder

upon the sand

as full-moon tide

roars closer,

bringing with it

precious life and

splintered shells

in holy rhythms of

living and dying,

wrapping each gift

in intricate beauty.

SILVER CRESCENDO

Dark shadow glides just beneath
     the water's surface,
Pacing itself in steady motion.

Another creature,
     lurking deep,
Makes his feisty move,
     seeking his dinner.

Unheralded, the startled mass
     explodes
To become a jumping eruption of
     popping silver.

Fish! Leaping!
Flying out of the water
     in frenzied escape.

With a brilliant flash
Life becomes a chase—
Wild and glorious!

And the fragile line marking
     life and death
Startles me with Reality.

OUR WAITING GOD

O God, you stand at the
window of my heart,
and you wait.

As close as my very breath,
You wait.

When my heart is …
       closed
       walled
       locked
you will not enter.

Blocked and rejected,
uninvited or unwelcome,
You will not come in.

Oh, but you wait!
Ceaselessly,
you long for me.

How near you are,
even when my heart
is tightly shut
within me.

And as you wait,
you know that
I will call to you again.

One day.

FINDING GOD

Hushhh ... Hushhh.
Listen to the quiet.
Soundless space.
No drone of motor.
No din of machinery.
No blast of music.
No singing creature.
No spoken word.
Stillness covers all, save the
Single quaking leaf stirring gently
And the solitary monarch that
Glides in silence.
Shhh.
Do you hear it?
Listen again.
This is where God is today.

NIGHTTIME PEACE

Glimmer of shine pierces
The black-night leaves.
All is still.
No movement.
No breath of breeze.
Only slim-line moon
And a solitary star, a pin-dot of light,
Peek behind the leafy boughs.

How I love the night sky
With its palest pinks and
Lavenders lingering still
In the western heavens.

Cricket chorus shouts its music
As I watch the falling darkness
And stretch to glimpse
The sliver of moon
With its companion star
Along their nighttime journey.

The sky is so vast—and I?
Barely a speck,
Sitting in the stillness,
In wonder,
Here on the planet we call Earth.
Simply looking.

The world feels right this night.
I reach out and kiss the moon!

~ FRAGMENTS ~

And the daughter lamented, "My life is a mess. I am constantly being interrupted in all things I intend to accomplish. I seem unable to follow through with any plans. I lose my direction. Nothing is completed!"

And the Father said, "My child, I am in the interruptions. Look for me there."

Disorder

swallowing my day,
paper mountains greet me from
every vacant space

such a noble goal—
to pare down the exploding
debris that looms here

window beckons me
to stand and gaze as I run
from my dreaded tasks

surely I may die
no further along than now,
praying for mercy

On Retirement

a delicate line
separates contentment
from boredom.
the space I sought
between frenzy
and quiet is a
downward plunge.
in the gap hangs
only a void.
when energies generated
by deadlines and decisions,
issues and commitments
are no more,
all is blank.
where is my direction?
my drive? …
dispersed and fizzled.
and where are the friends?
the colleagues? …
scattered and gone.
and the downshift
brings to me
a restlessness
that disallows peace.
and in the uneasy space,
I work to readjust.
Again.

On Needing Wisdom

Lord, here I am again,
Struggling to see more clearly.
Ah, Lord, I have
Too many ideas,
Too many passions,
Too many plans.
And fatigue engulfs me!

Perhaps if I spent more time
In the follow-through,
In the doing
Rather than the brooding
And the stewing,
Exhaustion would not
Oppress me.

Grant me wisdom in my choosing
So as not to wear myself out
With selfish efforts to experience
And participate in and
Fix ...
Everything.

TEMPO

with incremental
precision the clock measures
our hallowed moments

segmenting our lives
into sleeping and waking,
dreaming and doing

pacing the rhythm
of life, time's precious treasure
must not conquer it

TIME AND MEMORY

Don't ask me where yesterday went.
It came and then suddenly fled,
Melting into today.

What did I do with the day?
There is no record.
Little things here and small things there
Grabbed my time and stole my attention.

A perplexity that leaves me wondering—
Which is the measure,
My "doing"?
Or my memory
Of "not doing"?

Where is the line
That separates
The ongoing flow
Of day into night
Into day again?
The mark that says,
"This was yesterday"?

LOST PRAYER

What happened to my prayer?
I was just so recently sitting here,
Absorbed in my heart's prayer,
But where is it now?
Something happened.
Some miscellaneous distraction,
I suppose.
Did you hear it, Lord?
Has it come to you?
Perhaps it merely dissipated into
A vaporous sigh.
Yet it is no longer here.
And so I move on, trusting
That in your great power
You have received what was
In my heart.
Ah, such is my life with you
These days.
So often it is only an
Interrupted prayer.

Prayer for Community

Dear God, I am so

Untethered
Disconnected
Free-floating
Suspended

And I long to be

Grounded
Anchored
Rooted
Attached

Lead me by your Spirit, O Lord.
Draw me unto your heart, O Lord.
Pull me to the place prepared for me, O Lord.

For my heart longs for communion,
To be held in your Holy Presence,
To rest in your grace.

So be it. Amen.

FINDING PEACE

Loose ends.
So many!
Unraveled.
Frayed.
How to stop
The shreds?
That is the issue.
Remember—
Out of the stopping,
Out of the stillness,
Out of the silence,
Out of the waiting—
This and only this
Is how I become
Centered.
This and only this
Is my way to
Peace.

JUST DO IT

Just do it for me, Lord.
I want you to
> open the door,
> pave the way,
> take my hand.

Just put me where you want me.
I'm tired of guessing
> and wondering
> and waffling.

Weary of waiting
> for signs
> for voices
> for neon arrows pointing the way.

Won't you just take over, Lord?
I'm tired.
Please, just do it—
> tell me.
> show me.
> lead me.
> push me!

Let me skip the struggle.
Let me go straight to my place.
I don't want
> the decisions
> the uncertainties
> the anxieties.

No more wrangling, Lord.
No more figuring it out.
No more trial and error.
No more wait and see.

I am ready, God!
Just plunk me down in the middle
        of your will
And I will live there
        happily ever after.

Amen!

~ LAMENT ~

"Then they cried out to the LORD in their trouble,
    and he brought them out of their distress.
He stilled the storm to a whisper;
    the waves of the sea were hushed."

Psalms 107:28–29 NIV

Lamenting is biblical. Just check out the book of Psalms or the prophets or pick most any story. Suffering comes with living. Jesus experienced this fully. And if you think about it, the Scriptures, both Old and New Testaments, are all about giving us permission to call out with passion to our God.

It is in speaking openly to God that our communion becomes deep, trusting. After all, God knows our hearts and minds anyway. When we are troubled, depressed, or angry, where else can we go but to our loving God? God who hears us and holds us and comforts us in all our days.

CRYING

My eyes spill over with salty tears.

How do you comfort the crying child
Who wails and sobs for her small treasure?

Such tears.
Such weeping.
Such sorrow.

The sand dollars,
Gathered from ocean's edge
By little-girl hands.
How precious to her!
Now lying crushed and broken
Into a myriad of tiny bits.

And I, too, cry
Because now she knows—
Her six-year-old heart now *knows.*
It tastes the hurt.
Inside her little self,
She feels the stabbing pain of loss,
And this vibrant, joyful child
Has encountered grief.

Much too young for this
discovery, I think.

And I weep with her.

My "Almost" Friend

I never knew her,
this woman of compassion
and devotion
whose brilliance shone
in godly service.

I wanted to know her,
for her face spoke
kindness to me,
but life went on
and busyness prevailed,
so I never knew her.

With startling swiftness,
her life shifted and
vibrancy became frailty,
health became infirmity,
and in God's great mercy,
it was over.

Resting now in God's
heavenly realm,
she is whole again,
but my sadness lingers
because I never knew her.

PERSONAL INTERVIEW

Will you let me cry?

can you allow my tears
to run freely,
pouring pain and joy?

will you catch them
in loving hands and
see the sacred life
contained within?

please hold me as I weep!

for if you will not permit
my tears, indeed
you will never know me.

Will you let me cry?

Flying Home

He sits beside me

on the soaring jet.

Quiet and calm,

he reads his book.

A good and gentle man

who understands me

not at all.

Though he believes he knows

my heart and soul,

there is so much

that escapes him.

Completely.

Letters in My Mind

In the stillness of early dawn,
I write letters in my mind.

Words come quickly
        when I think of you.
Thoughts of telling
        and teaching.
Prayers of my heart
        spoken in earnest
        to ones I love.
Worldly cares and gentle reminders
        of living,
        of being.

Things forgotten, mostly
        when the sun is full
        and the day is filled.
A call to remember to hold dear
        the blessings
        and the strengths
        and God's unmerited grace.

Phrases and sentences
        too precious to speak
        at midday,
yet savored and tendered
        in the silence of daybreak.

All sent to you on the
        wings of angels.
Hoping inside that you will
        know it is from me.

With love.

WORKING IT OUT

Tall and silent,
She's at it again.
The leaf blower, the weed eater,
The mower, the broom.

Clipping.
Sweeping.
Digging.
Planting.

She's working it out, you see.
Her grief.
Perhaps not really aware,
But she's working it out.

It was summer.
She looked for him.
Planned.
Anticipated.
Waited.

He never came.
He died.
Her son died.
He never came.

The sorrow of it all!
Her son …
He never came.

And now,
In the mornings of summer,
She works it out.
Blowing and
Sweeping and
Pruning and
Mowing and
Digging and
Planting.

Her son died, you see.

SPRING'S FURY

I weep for you, suffering one.
You whose losses mount,
whose brokenness intensifies
as earth's violent temper
respects neither
gender nor race,
poverty nor wealth,
just nor unjust.
I weep for you.

Dipping from the
murky-black sky,
a frenzy of
turbulence and ferocity
stripped you
of all things precious,
of all sense and feeling,
and there are no words.
I weep for you.

Your life lies littered
in the wasteland
stretched before you;
numbness,
the mysterious paralysis,
prevails.
And I weep for you.

No prayers form
on your lips—
only a whisper of the
deep cry of the ages,
"O God!"

And God weeps with you.

THE NEWS

Television, computer,
Telephone, newspaper.
Bullets of words and scenes
Bringing the almighty "news"
Into every eye and ear and
Sanctuary of rest.
Burning my ears
With scorching talk;
Stinging my eyes
With visual horror.

Daily and hourly it
Pounds my brain with
Unsolvable problems.
Over and over it
Pierces my heart for those
I cannot help.

No more, please!
No longer can I bear
Its barrage of high-pitched words
Or view its offensive
And violent images
All seeking to make
A home in my mind.

Some days, I just want
To live in my little box.

Please.

JUST NOT READY TO DIE

My body speaks of things gone wrong.

Something sensed but yet unnamed.

Spinning thoughts overtake my mind

as fear and reason wrestle

for top-dog billing,

launching the anxious decision

to make the call or ...

to wait.

And all the while my silent voice cries,

Lord, I'm just not ready to die!

SENSITIVE HEART

Don't touch my heart.
There's hurt in there,
So back away, please.
Just tiptoe around the edges.

Let me do my tasks—
The diligence of keeping order,
The daily maintenance,
The necessary duties.

But don't come to my heart.
It is the center place.
The gathering place
Of all my wounds—
The losses, the memories,
The rejections, the disappointments.

And I haven't got time
To drag it all out.

So please,
Just don't touch my heart.

Heart Wall

He has a wall around his heart.
Hard.
Cold.
Stone.

The saddest thing I know
is living life
with a wall
around your heart.

Working so hard to keep
things inside
that need to
come out.

Working so hard to keep
things outside
that need to
come in.

It's fear, I think,
that makes this so.

But, oh, what senseless
effort it takes
to live with a wall
around your heart!

THE TEARS

Tear by tear,

the hurt falls away

as streams of pain

run down my cheeks,

emptying my aching heart

to create a space

for your loving touch.

O Christ, come in.

Come and heal

the place of anguish.

Soothe the pool

of my gathered tears,

and let your spirit

hold me.

THROUGH THE SHADOWS

as spirit breezes toss the leaves,
shining Light peeks through
and warms my cold pain
with loving assurance of
grace and peace

how powerful is this single ray
that forms behind the shadows
of today's despair
and covers me in my
woundedness.

~ The Cell ~

"Go, sit in your cell and your cell
will teach you everything." (Abbot Moses)
—Thomas Merton, *The Wisdom of the Desert*

The cell. A place of quiet. Closed door. Just you and God.
Alone. Together. Silent. Place of communion. Away from
distractions. Go! God will meet you there.

SACRED SPACE

Funny, Lord,
for me to be here on this
rather wild piece of ground,
hidden inside the city.

Only the muffled roar of traffic
and fleeting glimpse of
camouflaged rooftops
tell me of things outside
this rugged lakeside sanctuary.

The Cell in the City.

"Come in," it calls.
"Step into the quiet
and listen for a time.
Leave your clanging,
shouting day and
join me in stillness.
Wait for me here,
for I will find you—
only to release you
again to attend to your
noisy, tumultuous life.

But you will be changed."

THE DILEMMA

I pray for wisdom,
but on the heels of wisdom
comes courage,
and I am afraid
to ask God
for courage.

For if I pray for courage,
God may grant it, and
then the chaos would
begin and spill over
into everyone's life
with bitterness and old
wounds and hurts spewing
onto children and parents
and brothers and sisters.
Then where would be
the Good?

Healing cannot come without
a cost, but I just don't think
I am ready to pay the price.
This corner where I stand
is squeezing me, and
no answer comes,
save wisdom and courage—
my prayer dilemma.

WILDERNESS TIME

I've lost my inspiration.
All is dry these days, and I hear
no word from the Lord.

It must be my wilderness time,
For I am wandering through
barren and thirsty land
where there is no water.

So now, O Lord, what shall I do?
No sweet and tender words
flow from my mouth,
And no loving goodness
pours from my soul.

Is this how it will be?
Am I to roam this desert forever?
O God, this is so hard,
For I am unused to such
drought of spirit,
hollowness of feeling.

My soul longs for food,
For the days of love and beauty
And words and wisdom
bubbling to the surface,
overfilling my days.

Come quickly, Lord!
While I wander in this wasteland,
Teach my soul
>   to go deeper for water,
>   to trust for rescue,
>   to wait with hope
>   as long as it takes.

As long as it takes.

NOT READY

I'm just not ready, Lord.
Can't open the door.
Not even a crack.
"Do not enter"
Is the sign I wear.
To say "Come in"
invites dependency,
acknowledges not knowing,
surrenders control.
I must remain—
Independent. Self-sufficient.
All-knowing. All-controlling.
Completely in charge.
Entirely capable. Totally together.
Perfect in every way.
I'm just not ready, Lord.
You see, I'm not quite sure
who I am or
who I would become.
Open the door?
Too scary!
So … Shut it tight!
Lock it up!
"Stay out!" I say.
But in my fear,
I can never know you.
I can only continue
Locking more doors.

A Deteriorating Scene

It was a lovely day until
I blew it.
I allowed hurting words
to wound me.

A dangerous thing—
hurt turned fiery,
exploding into anger.

How frightening for
the volcano to erupt
with such ferocity;
so quickly the spewing!
It scares me.

So much power in
the little words
that spilled out!

Now I am the one
who is unforgiven,
and the pain of that
crushes me.

No resolution.
No rescue.
I remain bruised
and weary, just
needing forgiveness.

Fire and Forgiveness

Burn away my sin.

Refine the edges
    of my heart.

Purify my soul and my flesh
    with your blaze

That I may once again
    stand straight
    walk confidently
    live boldly

In the power of
    your mercy
    your love
    your grace.

LITANY OF LOVE

O Lord, I am unworthy.

You love me anyway.

O Lord, I am inadequate.

You love me anyway.

O Lord, I am so weak.

You love me anyway.

O Lord, I often wander far from you.

You call me back and love me anyway.

O Lord, I am sick—
    I am tired—
    I am unable—
    I mess up—

O gracious God, you love me anyway!

Hallelujah! Amen.

The Poor

ah, the poor!

always present

and yet

not always visible.

we like them unseen.

for to see them

is to encounter them.

to encounter them

is to care.

and when we care,

our tears flow freely,

and we begin

to love

and

to give.

then we are the ones

who are blessed.

ON BEING WHERE GOD IS

I saw you today, Lord.
I have been looking for you
for quite a while, you know.
I thought you might
be here, for this is
where you like
to hang out, I think.

And today, I saw your face;
today, I heard your voice.
In the eyes of James and Peggy
and Robert and Shirley
and Mary and Henry,
I saw your eyes.

And whenever these,
your children, spoke,
I heard your voice—
clear and honest,
plain and kind.

And you fed my
hungry soul.

ABOUT THE LOVING

Ah, Holy Lord,
it isn't about my
doing or accomplishing
or working or producing
or thinking or speaking.

It is only about
the *loving.*

Loving the insolent driver,
loving the slick politician,
loving the ugly one,
the disfigured one,
the arrogant one.

All you really ask of me
is to love these,
your own dear ones,
in the same way that
you love *me*
When *I* am ...

       arrogant
       or rude
       or selfish
       or ugly.

That's all, Lord.

That's all.

WARM ME FROM THE INSIDE

Funny how summer's swelter can cause
My skin to sweat with discomfort,
Yet my inside heart remains ice-coated.

And how winter's chill can cause shivers
Around my body, but within,
My heart may be soft and warm.

I think it is God whose Spirit inside me
Melts the ice and softens
My stony heart.

So when I drink my morning coffee,
I say a prayer and ask God this day
Just to ... warm me from the inside.

VORTEX

inexplicable force
of swirling power
encircles me
with waves.

I move with
the currents.

abruptly
it drops me,
and I sink
into the chair.

my breath becomes
paramount,
and I am silent,
sitting now in
perfect stillness.

pondering.

Amen.

WATERWORKS

O water my soul!

Nourish my heart with your words.

Let my mouth speak beauty

And my fingers write wisdom.

For your Voice will come upon me

Like a waterfall

Pouring down over my head.

Cleansing.

Revealing.

Restoring my life.

And I shall rejoice

In the drenching.

~ DARKNESS AND LIGHT ~

Sweet holy darkness
wraps me up in its whisper
when too bright light screams.

INTO THE DARKNESS

I sink into the abyss,

the swallowing darkness

where Christ reaches down to

Save.

Rescuing me from

the spinning blackness,

Jesus catches my

Soul,

setting me squarely

inside the shaft of

Light

where I am loved.

ESCAPE

Tonight I seek the
Holy Dark.

The sacred darkness of
your quiet,
your peace.

Away from daylight's
din of voices,
blare of sounds,
blinding glare.

The warmth of dark—
ah, your deepest heart.

Let me enter
into that space.

The soft nest of protection
wrapping me in a silent cushion
of warmth,
of safety.

The Holy Darkness.
Far beyond myself.

Drawn by Love into the deep heart
of your grace
to rest.

Dark Peace

I think I've found a sacred space
tucked inside the forest room
behind the oaks and pines and myrtle
where I listen to the night sounds, unseen.

Misty darkness creeps up to me,
and I melt into the chocolate nighttime,
sweet and dark and intense.

Blending into dusky evening,
the shadowy shoreline
heightens my senses
in the mystic stillness.

Hush of enveloping blackness stalks,
and my eyes are opened to the holiness
of the approaching night.

I sit in silence as
warm blackness touches
my skin, and I know with certainty
that I have become invisible.

THE FLAME

I wonder how it is
      that I have overlooked
      the candle capturing my eye
        just now.

With mystical power, the solitary flame
      beckons and pulls my whole being
        into its tiny light.

In other times,
      demanding agendas
      permitted only a glance from me,
      a nod of acknowledgment,
        and then dismissal.

How is it now that this
      bending,
      waving firelight
      engages me so
        and bids me stop?

And in the hushed stillness,
      I become pensive,
      warmed and nourished by
        the Mystery of it all.

A Prayer

I want to sit in the light.

I want to feel your fire.

I want to sense your glory.

I want to absorb your love.

Rest on me, O Light of Christ.

Enter my heart and abide within.

Warm my soul.

Heal my body.

Give strength to my spirit.

Amen.

Moon Walk

If you've never
walked at night,
you've missed the
moonbeam bath
that softly illumines
you and all things
so that the pure blackness
does not swallow you
down its dark hole.

Then moon-shadows
reveal the truth about
Light in the Darkness,
and now you can see it,
and now you can know it,
and in this knowing,
your walk turns into a dance
under the shining moon.

Evening Prayer

So tired.

Send your angels

To guard my sleep.

The darkness tonight

Wraps me in softness, and

I can rest in its

Silence.

Hold me, Lord,

In your love.

Whisper to me your peace,

O Spirit of Truth.

Let morning break

The night into day,

And send me out anew

In your

Shining Presence.

~ Haiku ~

This Japanese form of poetry contains brief expressions of a transient awareness of something observed, traditionally in the natural world. I love the succinctness of these "little lines" that give such precise structure to thoughts.

Haiku can sharpen one's perceptions of any simple object, truth, or discovery. It captures the moment. Haiku stops us—slowing us down in a way that can lead more easily into a period of calm or meditation. And, sometimes, there may even be a story.

~

"Then he said to me, 'Son of man, eat this scroll I am giving you and fill your stomach with it. So I ate it and it tasted as sweet as honey in my mouth.'"

—Ezekiel 3:3 NIV

And [in haiku] the Lord said:
"Eat these words of mine.
Taste them; chew them; swallow them.
Then you shall know truth."

INVOCATION ...

Call the dawn, O God,
And open the day for me
To welcome your love.

Come, Holy Spirit.
Fill the spaces of my life
With holy surprise!

Joy ...

Like a thousand bells,
Yellow leaves shake in the wind,
Ringing hushed music.

Bless me, O music!
Let me live your rhythmic joy
And clap holy hands.

WONDER ...

clarion singing
welcomes morn as tiny wren
offers his pure voice.

two white tails gleaming
as big-eared fawns run in fear
while I stand frozen.

giant orb rises,
pouring yellow through tree leaves
in the muted dawn.

red moon hanging low,
breaking over eastern sky,
inviting romance.

soupy fog swallows
the ground in misty secrets,
hiding earth and sky.

ocean meeting sky
whispers awe
in sacred language.

where sea touches sky,
mystery
creates a thin place.

STORMY DAY ...

wind-whipped rain drenches
surfaces already soaked
by the wild torrents.

rolling storm rumbles
as pieces of gray linger.
slits of sun slip through.

THE OAK ...

live oak twists and bends
from trunk outward in spirals,
unlike palm or pine.

stately grace abounds
in magnificent branches
and strength of bent limbs.

majestic arching
stretches to encircle Earth
like God's strong embrace.

SWEET HOT SUMMER ...

listen to the drone
of cicadas in August.
hot summer music.

under cover of
lavender sky at sunset,
summer creatures sing.

COFFEE ...

coffee in my cup
awakening sleepy mind,
warming chilly heart.

Katie's Breakfast ...

single blueberry
resting in milky-white bowl,
looking quite lonely.

DELIGHT ...

each child a rainbow
that lights and colors the world
with diamond starshine.

waves tickle her toes
as soft and shimmering sand
sinks beneath her feet.

thank you, God, for smiles,
for bursting-out-loud chuckles
and booming guffaws!

AGING ...

unfolding rosebud
stretching to the brightest light,
soon with faded bloom.

WATCH OUT ...

Politics defames
The truth of the living God.
Evil lurks in lies.

In silence and stealth,
Satan creeps in like a cat.
I see him and run.

Bitter root divides
And splinters all that is Love,
Leaving us weeping.

A healthy body
That fails to nourish the soul
Remains a cripple.

A rootlessness nags
When there is no Sabbath rest.
Peace comes with stopping.

It's not the big fire
That pleases God, but rather
The small flame of love.

Advice ...

Too much passion
Sears the heart's wisdom,
Scorching the senses.

Learn to tiptoe out
Of the scene and gaze broadly
For a clearer view.

Wisdom ...

Wisdom is silent.
A loose tongue heaps up trouble
With mindless flapping.

It is a wise man
Who knows that he does not know.
The humble find truth.

He who seeks wisdom
Listens to words of others
And sifts them with care.

Good-byes ...

good-byes were uttered
with perfunctory duty,
and we're still broken.

voicing our farewell
touched a hollowness of heart
that remains unhealed.

STRUGGLES AND PRAYER ...

Through pain and despair,
They wander the lonely road,
Longing for the Light.

In the holy quiet,
She endures with courage and
God wraps her in stars.

ALLIGATOR STORY ...

dead alligator
belly-up in the water,
quietly removed.

who knows the story
of this impressive creature's
untimely demise?

BROKEN PIECES ...

Torn and shredded hearts
long for the peace of healing,
the calm of wholeness.

I, too, am broken,
yearning for warm compassion
that mends fractured scraps.

Weave me together;
take these slivers of myself
and knit a whole cloth.

Then love's rich beauty
will encircle my shoulders
with inward caress.

SILENCE ...

with a fury like
swarming bees, our endless tasks
hide the heart's silence.

yearning for stillness,
barren souls beg for quiet,
yet we do not stop.

respite from the world
calls us to silent retreat
though we do not heed.

distracting ourselves
with lesser things fails to heal,
and we waste away.

stopping brings silence
and moves the soul from jangling
fragments to wholeness.

THE BIRD ...

Solitary bird
Sits alone on the dead limb,
Brooding and waiting.

I am the lone bird,
Wondering whether to fly
Or simply to rest.

Spirit of Truth come
And touch me with courage that
I may fly boldly!

THE SHEPHERD ...

lost and wandering,
a sinner, poor and needy,
I come now to you.

the tender Shepherd
comes to me, loves me, saves me
from my wilderness.

just knowing his love
soothes my anxious spirit and
covers me with peace.

Your Voice ...

Serenity falls
upon the shoulders of one
who holds the silence.

O Lord, speak to me
in the ebb and flow of tide
and the rush of wind.

Let me hear your voice
in ev'ry bird's melody
so I, too, may sing.

~ CIRCLES ~

Think for a moment about circles. We speak of "going around in circles." There are "circles of faith" and the "circle of life"; layers of "concentric circles" and "spiraling circles." At last, we come "full circle" when we recognize that we have arrived at a place where the end is actually the beginning.

In Celtic Christianity, the circle speaks of God's encompassing love, protection, and grace. The simple prayer "Circle me, Lord" speaks of our own helplessness and is a petition for God to hold us in God's great love and protection.

Smooth and bending;
No beginning;
No ending.
Nonlinear and
Directionless
Save the seamless
Meeting where
It began.

"And the end of all our exploring will be to arrive where we started and know the place for the first time."
—T. S. Eliot, *Little Gidding*

BIG AND SMALL

Black Crow swoops and dives,
circles and loops;
closes in, backs away, then
sweeps in to make his point.

Brown Hawk sits stalwart, strong.
Steadfast red-tail ignores the irritant,
looking forward;
minding his business.

All the while, Black Crow
does his diving dance,
hoping to get a response
from one so ...
    still.
    confident.
    unruffled.

In a flash, Brown Hawk spreads
giant wings and soars on the wind,
leaving small crow making his
circle-spins around ...
    nothing.

Endings and Beginnings

Another year.
Days flow one into the other
like a river flowing over rocks,
always changing, yet familiar.

We cannot go back.
There is no returning to the origin,
only the awareness of
the source within.

Flowing particles of water,
time, and space continue as
day follows night and night
follows day again and again.

So here we are today,
a new place, though
knowing this is where
we have been before.

O Lord, you are our constant,
the Source of all life—
the running river
that binds us into One.

Airplane Window

Speeding over this
green ball,
cloud pillows
begin to bulk
beneath me in
thick bumps
of gray and white
while horizon's dome
stretches to the
highest reaches
of heaven,
and I cruise in this
thin place
between earth and sky
and ask,
"Are you there, God?"
With a stream of
sweet warmth,
your assuring power
enters my soul
through this
narrow window
by my side,
telling my heart …
"Here and everywhere."

The Birthday

Today I drink from the
     Birthday Cup.
Every sip a nectar of bittersweet
     memories and reflections.

From delights and fears of
     childhood's simplicity
     through adolescent turbulence
     to treasured scenes of
     weddings, births, and family.

Forever images of people and places—
     words spoken,
     issues confronted,
     love given,
     love received.

All a whirling dance of
     accolades and accomplishments
Intertwined with longings of heart
     and disappointments of spirit.

Life lived.
Deaths encountered.
Joy and sorrow.
Frenzy and peace.

I swallow the spicy liquid
     and remember.
With each taste, my soul is
     enriched.
With each breath, I am
     grateful.

Quiet Is the House

Quiet is the house.
No tiny voices whispering
little secrets or wailing big demands.
No stomping feet or kicking legs
bouncing and dancing
in childhood's crazy rhythm.
No giggles and smiles
squelched by big bear hugs
after the games and the ice cream.
The counters are clean now.
Not a single crumb today.
Cakes and pies and cereal and carrots—
all are gobbled and gone.
No milk. No fruit. No meat. No bread.
Bowls and plates and spoons and forks
and cups and glasses unending
are washed and stacked in order.
Empty is the table.
Empty are the beds.
Just two of us now,
holding our memories.
Alone.
Quiet.
Ah!

NINETY-ONE

My mother is a star.
She steals the show.
I see her broadly now
that other adoring ones
are present.
Her stories.
Her twinkling laughter.
Her captivating manner.

At ninety-one, she has us all
in the palm of her hand.
Raptly, we lean toward her,
afraid to miss the joke—
the punch line.

And with hearty delight,
we all fall down laughing
in synchronistic hilarity!

MOTHER'S VISIT

Mother is here.
Frail now.
Different from before
when she walked
confidently on her
ninety-four-year-old legs.

A walker guides her steps
as insecurity steals
her confidence.
Another adjustment, yet
still her words come quickly,
spoken with flair and
argumentative wit.

Even now,
I cannot out-think her.
Near blindness quickens
her mind as she diligently
nurtures every thought
behind failing eyes.

And what thoughts lie
behind her façade?

Plenty!

… and I know that I will
never win the
argument.

The Farewell

The memory of words
      spoken in haste
And the absence of
      words unsaid
Sting my heart with pain
      in this singular good-bye.
What is this busyness, this preoccupation
      with external affairs
That allows us entry only as far as the
      outer circle while
The scarcely noticed clock continues
      its ticking in steady rhythm?

In a flash of seemingly rapid
      acceleration, our time is up.
The hurrying of our departure abruptly
      concludes the visit, unfinished,
Brought to an end before its
      completeness.

Only the periphery was skirted
      as the clock ticked,
Rendering the interior circle
      empty, longing for a touch.
And I cry every time I leave you,
      needing more.

ETERNAL ASSURANCE

Shake off your fear!

Let peace be in your heart—
        the quiet calm,
        the soft assurance
That God is beside you,
        surrounding you,
        within you.

Christ is reaching for your hand.
This Jesus who has prepared
        your very space,
        your heart's true home,
        whose Spirit now envelops you.

Your place has been made ready.
It is there.
Waiting for you.
Perfect in beauty and welcome.

When it is time—
Only when it is time,
The loving hand of Jesus will touch
        your own.
And when your soul and body
        relinquish this mortal life,
You will stretch to clasp his hand.

And Christ will embrace you,
        lovingly.
His Light of all lights
will carry you to the place
of eternal healing and peace.

And, fully whole again,
you will soar on the wings of angels!

When it is time.

A VISION

Radiant rays of
Glory-light
Stream through
Sky and cloud.

Leaves shine golden
In the glint of
Yellow beams,
Swirling round and round,
Covering the road
Ahead of me.

Someone I know,
One I love,
Moves through the
Gold-kissed leaves
Glowing in the
Gleaming sun.

One I love is
Walking into the Light
Along the
Streets of Golden leaves.

Life's Celebration!

Clowns are tumbling,
Fireworks cracking—
There are flying kites
And red balloons,
Fresh strawberries
And peach ice cream,
Bacon frying
And popping corn,
Blueberry pie
And chocolate dreams,
Loving hugs and
Gentle words—
Thank you, God,
For gifts so good!
It all worked out and
Tensions fled,
Refreshed us all and
Souls were fed.
Let's jump and clap
And shout out loud
With hip-hooray
And woo-hoo-hoo.
We'll sing and dance
Our Hallelu!

CPSIA information can be obtained at www.ICGtesting.com
Printed in the USA
BVOW031740021012

301964BV00002B/4/P